Quick and Fun Learning Activities for Five-Year-Olds

Julia Jasmine, M.A.

Teacher Created Materials, Inc.

Cover Design by Larry Bauer

Illustrated by Jose L. Tapia and Sue Fullam

Order Number TCM 558

Table of Contents

Introduction

Leaving the Nest

Most five-year-old children are either in kindergarten or getting ready for the experience. Some may have been in pre-school for years. Others may be leaving the nest for the first time. Whatever the situation, it is an exciting time for both you and your child.

Print

Since the advent of television, our world has become so visual that almost all five-year-old children are aware of print—written language—in one form or another. Most of them also recognize the connection between print and the oral language it symbolizes. Television has actually increased this awareness because shows such as *Sesame Street* and *Barney* deliberately demonstrate the connection by teaching both the names of the letters and their phonetic sounds. Even the shows that are not consciously educational reinforce this connection because the commercials that children love contain lots of written words which are usually shown together with the spoken language they represent. If you read when your child is around, if you make and consult shopping and "to do" lists, and especially if you have been reading *to* your child, this connection between print and language has had an opportunity to develop even further.

Writing

Gaining control of the large and small muscles will make writing easier. Children should be encouraged and praised for trying to draw the alphabet letters with crayons. No matter how well they know the letters and can form them with manipulative materials, such as pipe cleaners and craft sticks, they need to practice using their fingers to hold the writing implement and trying to write the letters. This is hard work, but once it is mastered, life becomes much easier for a five-year-old.

Writing *(cont.)*

Turning print awareness into actual reading and writing is the major task your child will be undertaking in the next year or so. Since success in school often depends on reading and writing skills, any help you can give your child along these lines will really pay off. The best advice—read with your child daily!

Acquiring Social Skills

Becoming socialized, or acquiring the skills necessary for getting along in our society, is important, too. If your child knows about getting dressed and using the bathroom, and has basic table manners, people will enjoy having him around. If your child knows about crossing streets carefully and not talking to strangers, he will be relatively safe. If your child is able to share, take turns, say "please" and "thank you," and be quiet in a library, he will have taken the first steps toward being well-liked in the classroom by the teacher and classmates alike.

All of these skills are best learned through experience. Skill in getting dressed, using the bathroom, and eating politely occurs when children have performed the actions often enough to become comfortable with them. Safety skills need to be practiced over and over in low-key, stressless situations. Children, whether or not they have other children to play with, learn to share, take turns, and say "please" and "thank you" because that is how things are done in their families. And the only way anyone can learn to be quiet in a library is to go to one often.

Building a Knowledge Base

Learning to read and write and becoming socialized depend on acquiring a great deal of general information, a kind of knowledge base to fall back on and use. This is also a memory-training device of sorts, based on repetition and practice.

Introduction *(cont.)*

Building a Knowledge Base *(cont.)*

Children will be happier at this age if they know their full names and addresses, telephone number and birth dates, their parents' or guardians' names and what they do, including their places of employment and daytime telephone numbers.

Children will be more secure if they have used a telephone by themselves and if they can show you (or tell you) how to get from school to home. It also helps if they know and feel comfortable with some of their neighbors. Show them where they live on a city street map. They like to see where they live pointed out on a U.S. map, too.

The world, especially school, will be a friendlier place if five-year-olds know the names of the colors and numbers, if they can tell which are their right and left hands, if they have been exposed to the concepts of opposites and rhyming words, and if they have played with and used materials such as sand and water.

Computers are part of a child's world now. If you have access to one, make sure your child has a chance to use it. Just knowing where the space bar and enter or return keys are will provide a child entering kindergarten with a great deal of self-confidence. It will be a bonus if he has become familiar with the keyboard and can enter his name.

Communicating

The activities that follow will fit naturally into parts of almost any child's day and help you as a parent to provide the experiences your child needs to develop print awareness, social skills, and general knowledge. If you read them over ahead of time, you will be able to implement them naturally. They will become a spontaneous part of the communication you share with your child.

Your Five-Year-Old

Too Big or Too Little

Depending on the regulations of your school district and the month in which your child was born, your five-year-old might be "too big" for pre-school or "too little" for kindergarten. Much of a five-year-old's life falls into those two categories—too big to do the "baby" things that are still appealing, and too little to do the "big kid" things that are so attractive. What does a five-year-old need?

Meeting the Needs of a Five-Year-Old

- A five-year-old needs to develop in all areas—physical, cognitive, social, and emotional.
- A five-year-old needs to be physically active.
- A five-year-old needs real things to think about and activities that are concrete and hands-on.
- A five-year-old needs to interact and communicate with other children and with adults.
- A five-year-old needs to develop competence and have it recognized by others.
- A five-year-old needs adult help to develop a conscience and achieve self-control.
- A five-year-old needs adult support in building toward independence.

How to Use This Book

One Long Conversation

Life with a five-year-old should be one long, continuous conversation. Use this book to stimulate conversation with your five-year-old.

- Talk about "what" and "who."
- Talk about "when" and "where."
- Talk about "if" and "then."
- Talk about "how" and "why."
- Talk about "yesterday," "today," and "tomorrow."
- Talk about "last year" and "next year."
- Talk about cause and effect.
- Talk about colors, sounds, smells, and tastes.
- Talk about the kind of feeling you do with your fingers and the kind you do with your heart.
- Talk about the things you like, the people you love, and why.
- Talk about the things and the people you don't like and why.
- Talk about raindrops and snowflakes, sunrises and sunsets, the stars and the moon, puppies and kittens, and flowers and butterflies.
- Talk about yourselves, what you want and need, and what you hope and dream.
- Never stop talking!

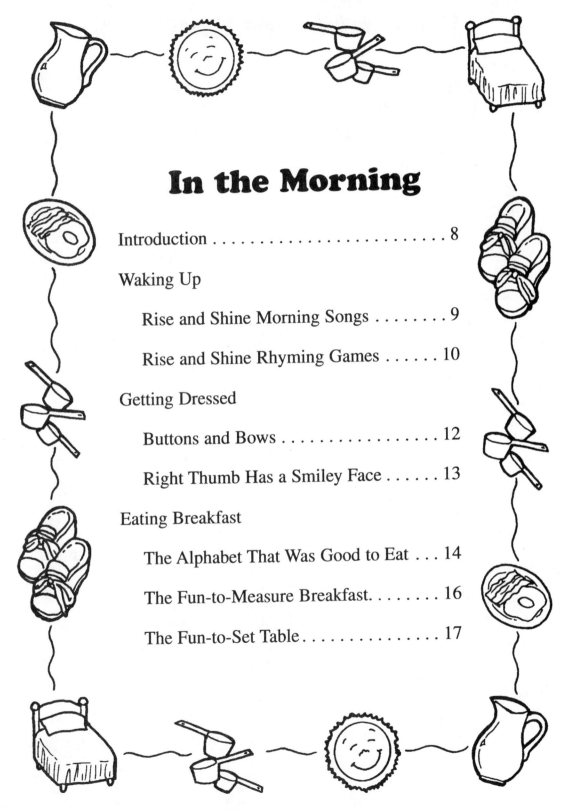

In the Morning

Introduction

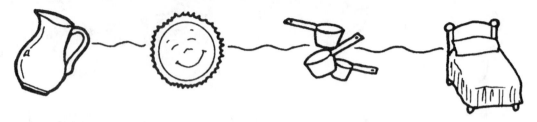

Be Prepared

Mornings can be awful times or wonderful times. If you can manage to make them wonderful, you will give both you and your child a great start for the day. Sometimes having an activity in mind the night before will help you to begin the next day on a positive note, especially if you have never thought of yourself as a "morning person."

Sometimes, even though it sounds awful, it helps if Mommy gets up a half hour earlier than everyone else. Have an extra cup of coffee, read the paper, write in a journal, meditate, whatever you feel like doing—but do it by yourself! This practice will refresh you for the day and make you feel as if you also have a life.

Make It Easier

The activities in this section have been designed to help make mornings easy and enjoyable by focusing on the areas that can turn into problems: waking up, getting dressed, and eating breakfast.

Waking Up

Do you and your five-year-old like to sing simple songs? If so, this is a great way to wake up your child.

Getting Dressed

Spontaneous rhyming games are fun, too. Anything that is light and whimsical will make the day look bright. This is a great time for creativity—anything goes because you have such a good audience.

Eating Breakfast

Try "The Alphabet That Was Good to Eat" or "The Breakfast That Was Fun to Measure." Make breakfast a time together in anticipation of a great day.

Rise and Shine
Morning Songs

Activities

Materials

• None

Teach your child the following song by singing it (to any tune that suits you) every morning over a period of time. When the words are very familiar, your child can act it out by going to the window to address the sun with the first verse. You can answer for the sun as the second verse. Later, you can reverse roles.

If your child has a globe, you can point out where you live, and when it seems appropriate, you can hold the globe near a lamp and demonstrate night and day by turning the globe.

Here Comes the Sun

Child:

Here comes the sun.
The sun wakes me.
Where have you been, sun?
What did you see?

Sun:

I never moved.
You went away.
Now, here you come
To start the day.

Good Morning to You

This is a song that is often sung to open the day in a primary or early childhood classroom, so some children will already know it.

Good morning to you
Good morning to you.
We're all in our places
With sunshiny faces.
Good morning to you.
Good morning to you.

Rise and Shine Rhyming Games

Materials

• None

Activity

Teach your child the following game by playing it for a few minutes every morning. It can be a waking-up game, a game that goes with getting dressed or eating breakfast, or just a rhyming game. Several groups of words, based on different themes, follow for your morning convenience.

I Say/You Say

Waking up

I say deep and you say _____.   sleep/peep

I say fawn and you say _____.   yawn/dawn

I say cup and you say _____.   up/pup

I say late and you say _____.   wait/date

I say rock and you say _____.   clock/sock

I say sight and you say _____.   light/bright

I say nosy and you say _____.   cozy/rosy

Rise and Shine
Rhyming Games *(cont.)*

Getting Dressed

I say letter and you say _____.   sweater/better

I say guess and you say _____.   dress/press/mess

I say dirt and you say _____.   shirt/Bert

I say means and you say _____.   jeans/beans

I say flocks and you say _____.   socks/blocks/rocks/fox

I say true and you say _____.   shoe/blue

Eating Breakfast

I say coast and you say _____.   toast/roast/most

I say toot and you say _____.   fruit/boot/suit

I say goose and you say _____.   juice/moose/loose

I say wham and you say _____.   ham/lamb/jam

I say stutter and you say _____.   butter/flutter/mutter

I say leg and you say _____.   egg/peg/beg

General Words

I say moon and you say _____.   noon/soon/tune/June

I say sun and you say _____.   fun/bun/run/ton

I say star and you say _____.   car/jar/mar/far

I say me and you say _____.   see/tree/be/he

I say town and you say _____.   brown/clown/frown/down

Buttons and Bows

Materials

- Old shoes
- Shoelaces
- Old shirts, sweaters, etc.

Activities

If your child's fingers are still having trouble with buttoning and unbuttoning or tying bows, keep the process of learning the skills separate from the morning rush. Say, "Here, let me help you," and button the buttons on her clothes and tie the laces on the shoes that are already on the feet. Then, when all is calm, do one of the following:

Try the Real Thing: Let your child practice lacing and tying, using a man's low-cut dress shoe and some thin laces that are easy to pull through the eyelets. Be ready to demonstrate tying a bow over and over. If you can't do this without becoming impatient, get someone else to do it or tape record your directions and let your child listen on earphones while lacing and tying. A tape can also be stopped, backed up, and replayed as often as desired. And it never becomes impatient or cross!

Provide a bag or basket of old sweaters, shirts, and jackets that can be buttoned and zipped any old time, without the additional pressure of getting dressed to meet a deadline. After a while, suggest that your child hold the garment so she is looking down at it to  make the practice more like the real thing.

Provide a Peer: Enlist the help of another child to teach these skills to your child. Children are much closer to the problems involved in the process of learning small muscle skills and often say and do just the right thing.

Right Thumb Has a Smiley Face

Materials
- Non-toxic marking pens

Activity

Some children seem to be born knowing which is their right and which is their left hand. Others are still putting their left hands over their hearts during the flag salute in the second grade. "And who cares?"—you may be thinking. Now that we know better than to try to change a left-handed child into a right-handed one, what difference does it make, after all, if a child can tell left from right? There are still a few times when left and right are important. We read and write from left to right, and it is important to know where to start. We use left and right when we give directions, such as "Turn left at the next corner." We put our left shoe on our left foot and our right shoe on our right one. If your child wants to remember, try this:

Using a non-toxic marking pen, draw a cute, smiley face on his right thumb every morning before he goes to school. One reassuring look at the happy thumb, and your child's problem with right and left is solved! You can do this as long as necessary, or continue as long as you want just for fun.

You can also draw a smiley face on the inside of your child's right shoe. Put the smiley shoe on the same side as the smiley thumb, and your child is off and running!

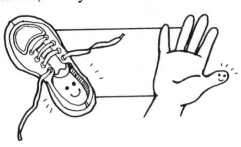

The Alphabet That Was Good to Eat

Materials

- Different kinds of food
- Paper tablecloths
- Paper placemats or construction paper
- Crayons or markers

Activity

Have a paper tablecloth or placemat on the table when your child sits down to breakfast.

Since this is an ongoing activity, you can stretch a letter over as many days as you wish. You can also model the activity on the first day and then let your child take over when she feels comfortable.

Start with the letter "A, a."

Serve at least one food starting with the "letter of the day," for example, an apple. (A list of suggestions follows.)

Think of as many foods as you can that begin with the letter of the day.

Play: "I went to the store and everything I bought began with (the letter of the day)."

With a crayon or marker, have your child cover the paper tablecloth or placemat with the letter of the day, using both upper and lowercase. You may wish to add a picture of a food item that begins with the letter of the day.

Decide on the letter for the next day.

The Alphabet That Was Good to Eat *(cont.)*

(You will undoubtedly think of many more.)

"**A**" is for almonds, apples, applesauce, apricots, artichokes, and avocados.

"**B**" is for bacon, bagels, bananas, beans, bologna, bread, breakfast, broccoli, buns, and butter.

"**C**" is for cake, carrots, cereal, cheese, chicken, cinnamon, cocoa, coffee cake, cookies, corn, cream, and cream cheese.

"**D**" is for dates, dinner, doughnut, and dumpling.

"**E**" is for eggs, eggplant, enchilada, and endive.

"**F**" is for fish, frankfurters, fries, fruit, and French fries.

"**G**" is for gingerbread, grapefruit, grapes, gravy, green beans, and green peppers.

"**H**" is for ham, hamburgers, honey, hot cakes, hash browns, and hot dogs.

"**I**" is for ice cream.

"**J**" is for jam, JELL-O, juice, and jelly.

"**K**" is for kale, ketchup, and kumquats.

"**L**" is for lemons, lettuce, limes, and lunch.

"**M**" is for macaroni, mangoes, marshmallows, mayonnaise, meat, milk, muffins, and mustard.

"**N**" is for nachos, noodles, and nuts.

"**O**" is for oatmeal, onions, orange juice, and oranges.

"**P**" is for pancakes, peaches, pears, peas, pickles, pie, pizza, potatoes, and pudding.

"**Q**" is for quince.

"**R**" is for radishes, raisins, and raspberries.

"**S**" is for salad, salsa, soup, sandwich, sauce, sausage, sherbet, stew, sweet potato, and syrup.

"**T**" is for taco, tamale, tea, tomato, tortilla, and turkey.

"**U**" is for upside-down cake.

"**V**" is for vegetables, vanilla, and vitamins.

"**W**" is for waffles, water, and watermelon.

"**X**" is for xanthophyll in corn, and what they eat in Xanadu.

"**Y**" is for yam, yeast, and yogurt.

"**Z**" is for zucchini and zwieback.

The Fun-to-Measure Breakfast

Materials

- Measuring spoons and cups
- Chart (See below.)

Activities

Give your child a ¹/₂-cup (120 ml) measure and ask him to add a cup of milk to the pancake batter (or whatever else) you are mixing. (Discuss what will need to happen before doing it.)

Repeat with a ¹/₃-cup (80 ml) measure and a ¹/₄-cup (60 ml) measure. (Discuss what will need to happen before doing it.)

Give your child a 1-pint (568 ml) measure and ask him to add about a cup of milk to some pudding mix.

Use your imagination to add to this list of other requests. Always try to use a measure that will make your child stop and figure out the answer. Examples include:

"Please pour 1 pint (473 ml) of orange juice into this pitcher."

"Jack wants another cup of milk."

"You can add 2 quarts (1.89 l) of water to the drink mix."

CHART

¹/₄ CUP + ¹/₄ CUP + ¹/₄ CUP + ¹/₄ CUP = 1 CUP
¹/₃ CUP + ¹/₃ CUP + ¹/₃ CUP = 1 CUP
¹/₂ CUP + ¹/₂ CUP = 1 CUP
1 CUP + 1 CUP = 1 PINT
1 CUP + 1 CUP + 1 CUP + 1 CUP = 1 QUART
1 PINT + 1 PINT = 1 QUART
1 QUART + 1 QUART = ¹/₂ GALLON

Reproduce this chart with a marker on construction paper and hang it in the kitchen for easy reference.

The Fun-to-Set Table

Materials

- Table settings
- Graphic representation (See next page.)

Activity

Enlarge the placemat on the following page and get several copies. On one or two of the copies, place a fork, spoon, knife, plate, and cup on the matching words and draw around them. Keep at least one copy with just the words. Laminate all of the placemats by covering them with clear contact paper so they can be used over and over.

Start by putting the prepared placemat (with the outlines of the tableware on it) on the table and letting your child place the silverware, plate, and cup right on the placemat.

When your child feels comfortable with this skill, have her use the placemat as a guide and set the tableware on the tablecloth or on another plain placemat.

Let your child try setting the table, using the placemat with just the words on it. Help with the words, if necessary.

The Fun-to-Set Table

CUP

SPOON

KNIFE

PLACEMAT

PLATE

FORK

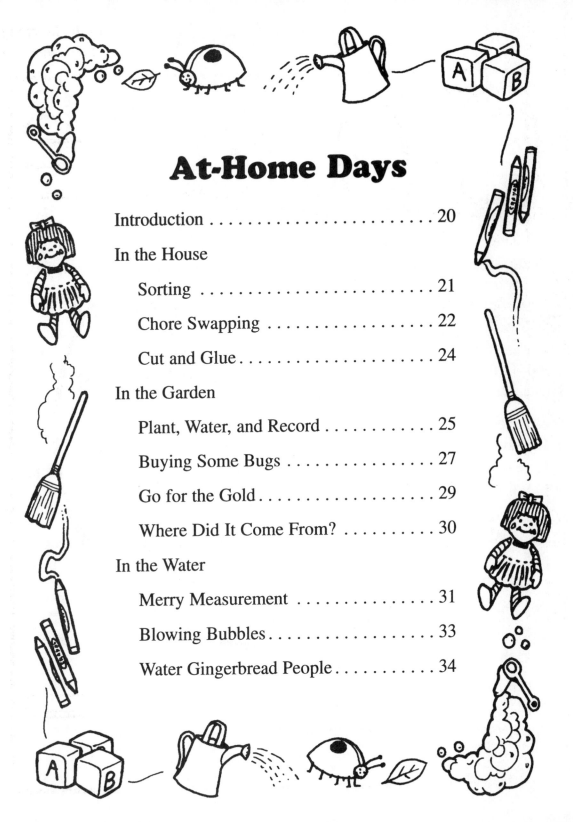

At-Home Days

Introduction

Special Days

Once your child starts the routine of school, he will have very few at-home days. These days can become very precious to him. He will look forward to them, and so can you, if you remember that you are making the memories your child will treasure when he is older.

An at-home day is a day when a child (and anybody involved with that child's care) does not have to go anywhere—no appointments, no errands, no lessons, no practices. An at-home day can be a breakfast-in-pajamas day, a lunch-on-the-deck day, or a very busy let's-clean-the-house-together day. The activity doesn't matter; it is the attitude that counts.

Make it Easier

The activities in this section have been designed to help make at-home days easy and entertaining by focusing on things that are already available, both indoors and outdoors.

In the House

Do all of the toys in your house have a million parts that have all become mixed up together? Believe it or not, sorting and picking-up games can be fun. So can cutting and gluing.

In the Garden

It is exciting to grow things. Whether you have a real garden, a planter on a deck, or a window box, you can plant, water, and pull weeds.

In the Water

Water play is always fun and you can do it in the bathtub, at the kitchen sink, or—in nice weather—in any outdoor area that is available.

Sorting

Materials

- Blocks
- Toys with lots of parts
- Buttons
- Coins
- Containers for grouping

Activity

Instead of saying, "Pick up your toys," try this. Collect a variety of containers: baskets, boxes, plastic tubs, etc. Make a few suggestions, such as, "Let's put all the wooden blocks in here, all the plastic blocks in here, and all the things that go with the tea set in here."

Encourage your child to sort things by attributes such as color, size, and shape. Start with one attribute and make the sorting more complicated as your child needs a greater challenge.

For example, you could use the following:
- Find all the red buttons.
- Find all the round red buttons.
- Find all the small, round red buttons.
- Find all the small, round, red, two-holed buttons.

You can sort all kinds of things you find at home. In addition to toys and buttons, try leaves, rocks, cards, books, coins, costume jewelry, cookies, candy, pictures cut from magazines, silverware, paper clips, etc. (This is a great way to get your desk drawers cleaned and organized, and your child will love to help!)

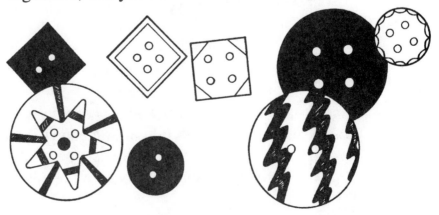

Chore Swapping

Materials
- A sense of humor

Activity

If your child doesn't already have some regular chores around your home, make a "Chore Chart" like the one on the next page, and use it for a period of time.

When you are ready to have a "Chore Swapping" day, discuss the idea with your child before you start: "Today I will do your morning chores while you do mine." But don't tell her what chores to do. The first time you do this activity, half the fun is getting a look at how your child sees you and what you do!

Set a timer, do the chores, and compare notes. (At this point, you can tell your child what else you do, if you want to.) Congratulate each other on jobs well done.

This activity is fun on a weekend at-home day when everyone is home. You can draw names and do the chores of different people in the family. This can lead to a very good discussion of what each person does and how all of the family chores contribute to everyone's happiness and well-being.

You might also want to consider some permanent chore swapping, especially if someone dislikes a particular chore. If everyone dislikes a particular chore, make it a revolving responsibility so no one is stuck with it forever.

Chore Swapping *(cont.)*

CHORE CHART

CHORE	S	M	T	W	T	F	S
Example: **Take out the trash**	Mom	Dad	Julie	Jimmy	Mom	Dad	Julie

Cut and Glue

Materials

- Large piece of plain, heavy paper
- Old magazines or catalogues
- Small paper rectangles
- Pens or markers
- Glue
- Scissors
- Large envelope

Activity

Even though the phonetic approach to reading is a useful and effective strategy, some five-year-old children do not have highly developed auditory skills. These children are helped a great deal by having a memory bank of sight words. They can use them until they are more comfortable with phonics. In fact, many children generalize from a sight vocabulary and use the words to enter into a phonetic approach as they suddenly "get" the idea that a sound in a word that they know is the same in another word they are trying to figure out.

Have your child browse through the magazines and catalogues and cut out (or mark for you to cut out) pictures that she knows the names of.

After the pictures are cut out, have her paste them on a large piece of paper (cardboard, poster board, or construction paper).

Point to each card in turn and ask your child the name of the picture. Discuss the pictures. Are these really "boots" or would "shoes" be a better name for the picture? Is this really a picture of just a slide, or does it show a whole playground?

After you have agreed on a name for each picture, print the word on a small rectangle of paper and put all the words in an envelope. Your child can then match the words with the pictures at any time she wants to play a quiet word game.

The game will soon become an independent activity, but you need to check every so often to see if the words are being matched correctly with the pictures.

Plant, Water, and Record

Materials

- Flower bed
- Planter or window box
- Garden tools
- Garden hose or watering can
- Plants and/or seeds
- Suitable clothes
- "Garden Chart" (See next page.)
- Colored pencils or markers

Activity

Check ahead of time to see if you have the equipment your child will need to plant things without too much adult help. Gather a supply of attractive seeds or buy some plants the day before you suggest this activity. (Remember, if you have to go out, it's not an at-home day.)

To get your child started, read the information on the seed packages aloud. Share your know-how about planting small plants. Show him how to water and how to stick markers in the soil to keep track of where the plants will come up.

Get some enlarged copies of the "Garden Chart" on the next page or use a blank calendar with large squares. Fill in the name of the month. Number the squares to match the days of your month. Show your child how to record information on the "Garden Chart" calendar. Try this method:

Use a different color of pencil or marker for each kind of seed.

Write an "X" on the day the seeds are planted.

Write a "W" each time the seeds are watered.

Write a "P" when the first plant appears.

Write an "F" for the first flower.

Plant, Water, and Record *(cont.)*

GARDEN CHART

_____

(month)

S	M	T	W	T	F	S

Buying Some Bugs

Materials

- Yellow Pages Phone Book
- Pencil
- "Record of Telephone Calls" (See next page.)

Activity

This is a very grown-up activity, one that will appeal to the five-year-old who aspires to acting like an adult.

In addition, this activity is one that will fit in with your child's developing environmental awareness. Many people who hesitate to use insect poisons in their gardens have learned to use helpful insects to eat the bad ones. This also makes it unnecessary to have poisons around the house that could pose a danger to your child.

Some of the helpful creatures available for purchase from most nurseries are ladybugs, praying mantises, nematodes, and snails.

Get your child ready for this activity by discussing garden pests and the harmful effects of using poisons to kill them.

Tell your child that the helpful garden creatures can be bought at nurseries and garden shops. Since this is an at-home activity, ask how she thinks you could find out about them. Once you have decided with your child to use the telephone for this activity, the excitement begins!

Help your child find the listings of nurseries and garden shops in the yellow pages of your phone book. They are usually listed as Nurseries—Plants, Trees, Etc.—Retail.

Select the ones you want to call and, using the "Record of Telephone Calls" on the next page, help your child write the names and telephone numbers on the appropriate lines.

Spend some time role playing before having your child make the real telephone calls. Coach her in the correct way to ask for information as you go along. Do it several times so the idea becomes familiar and comfortable.

Buying Some Bugs *(cont.)*

Record of Telephone Calls

Place called:_____

Telephone number:_____

Insects available: LADYBUGS   YES / NO $_____

PRAYING MANTISES   YES / NO $_____

Place called:_____

Telephone number:_____

Insects available: LADYBUGS   YES / NO $_____

PRAYING MANTISES   YES / NO $_____

Place called:_____

Telephone number:_____

Insects available: LADYBUGS   YES / NO $_____

PRAYING MANTISES   YES / NO $_____

Go for the Gold

Activity

Materials
• Pail or bag

Make a financial investment in your garden by sending your child on a dandelion hunt! Avoid spending hours digging out dandelions from your lawn and flower beds. Help your child earn extra spending money while doing a really worthwhile job!

Give your child a pail or a bag to collect yellow dandelion flowers in. (You might want to have the fluffy white ones collected, too, before the seeds have a chance to blow around, but it's better to catch them before they turn white.)

Tell your child you will pay (whatever you decide) for each dandelion and add this chore to his daily chore chart. (If you have an enormous lawn, you may want to pay a penny apiece for the dandelions; if you have a small garden, a nickel or a dime may be appropriate.)

Ask your child to count the dandelions each day. See if he can figure out how much money he has earned.

You might want to give your child a special bank for this dandelion money and plan for a celebration later in the year.

Other weeds and unwanted, nonpoisonous plant matter can be included, too. Some children become so enthused about earning money that they will spend long hours digging out crabgrass!

Where Did It Come From?

Materials

- *The Very Hungry Caterpillar* by Eric Carle
- Large glass jar with a lid
- Butterfly chrysalis and the piece of branch it was found on

Activity

Help your child to observe the caterpillars in your garden. Talk about the idea that they will soon turn into butterflies.

Read the book and/or view the video, *The Very Hungry Caterpillar* by Eric Carle. Most children like this story repeated over and over again.

When you begin to notice that the caterpillars are disappearing, help your child look for a chrysalis on a twig in your garden. Carefully detach the twig and place it, with the chrysalis still attached, in a terrarium or large glass jar. Cover the container with net or make enough holes in the lid to allow for good air circulation. Watch carefully, and when the butterfly begins to emerge from the chrysalis, uncover the container and place it outside or near an open door or window. Though it takes a couple of hours, observe with your child as the butterfly slowly stretches, moves its wings to strengthen them, and, finally, flies away.

Merry Measurement

Activity

Materials

- Unbreakable containers
- Water
- "Guess and Check Chart" (See next page.)
- Pencil or marker

This is a game that can be played in the bathtub, at the kitchen sink, or outdoors on a patio, deck, or grass area. Wear a swimsuit if the weather is warm, or have dry clothes ready to change into when the game is over.

Have your child select two containers—one large and one small—and make a guess as to how many small containers full of water it will take to fill the large one. (Containers like cups, bowls, pitchers, and tubs work well.)

Draw pictures of the two containers on an enlarged copy of the chart on the next page. Have your child guess how many small containers of water it will take to fill the large one and write her guess on the chart. Check by actually filling the small container and pouring the water into the large one as many times as it takes to fill it. Write this number on the chart next to the guess. Were you right? Play again. Try different combinations of containers.

Merry Measurement *(cont.)*

Guess and Check Chart

CONTAINERS	GUESS	CHECK

Blowing Bubbles

Materials

- Bubble liquid or baby shampoo
- Bubble wands or pipes
- Flat pans
- Water

Activity

This is a game that is best played outdoors on a patio, deck, or grassy area. Bubble liquid is very slippery, so be ready to hose off the deck or patio. The grass is actually the best place to blow bubbles. No cleanup is necessary! (You can also blow bubbles in the bathtub or at the kitchen sink, if some precautions are taken. Have your child sit down in the bathtub and put towels on the floor to keep from slipping.)

Bubble liquid can be irritating to the eyes. If your child's eyes are sensitive, make your own bubble liquid from any "no tears" baby shampoo. Try mixing it half-and-half (water and shampoo) and then see if you can dilute it further and still get good bubbles.

There are no rules for playing with bubbles. Make up games if you want to—you can see whose bubble is the biggest or flies the farthest or who can blow the most little bubbles. But it is just as much fun to simply watch the bubbles or run around and pop them. (Stay on the grass for the running part of this activity.)

This is probably the most relaxing activity in this book. Enjoy!

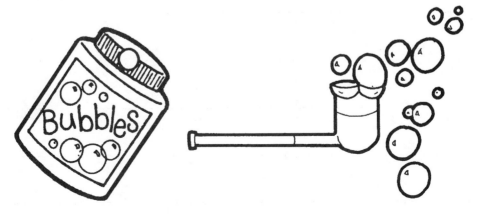

Water Gingerbread People

Materials

- An outdoor area
- Buckets for water
- Large paintbrushes
- Garden hose

Activities

These are definitely outdoor activities for warm or hot weather. You really need to be dressed in a swimsuit and have a fairly flat cement patio or sidewalk area to make them work. (*Caution:* Check to see that pavement is not too hot for this activity.)

You can think of these activities as a warm-climate substitute for snow. Children who have never made a snow angel can have some of the same kind of fun as those who live in cold-weather areas.

Fill your buckets with water and have your paintbrush handy. Have your child lie down flat and quickly paint around his outline with water. He must then jump up quickly and add facial features, buttons, and so on before the water evaporates. If you are playing, lie down and have your child paint around you. Giggling is expected!

A pleasant alternative for a really hot day is to use a hose and water your child with a fine light spray as he lies down on the ground. Continue as you did when painting. If you play, you will find it's as cooling as being in a pool.

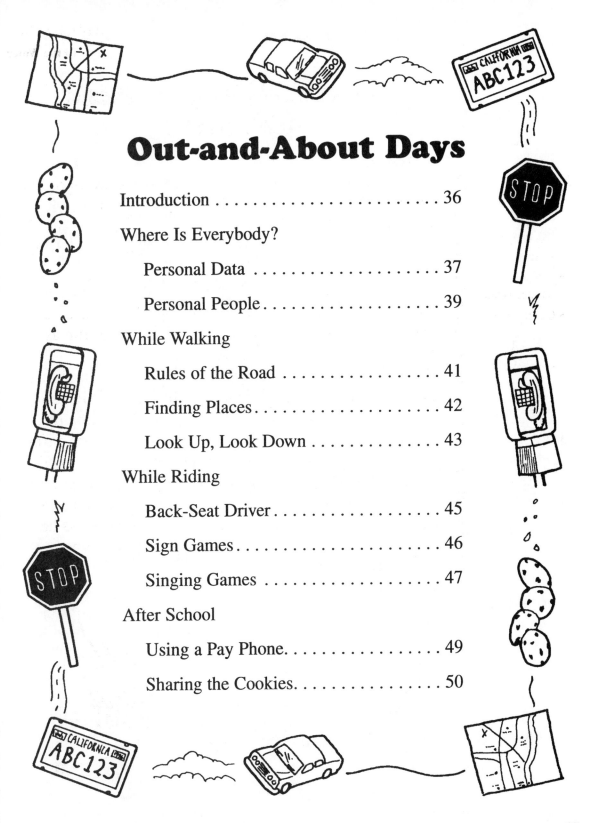

Out-and-About Days

Introduction

Ordinary Days

Unlike at-home days, out-and-about days are days when everyone has a lot to do and many places to go. You may be walking, riding a bus, or driving a car. However you are doing it, you are on the move. Five-year-olds tend to make hard work of moving along quickly to keep up with a schedule. They also find it hard to sit still in a car or bus. Out-and-about days can be difficult for everyone.

Since being out-and-about is a part of real life, it also affords a good chance to learn some real-life skills. If you can turn these learning experiences into pleasant activities, you will feel better, and you will also have a happier child. Just as with at-home days, it is the attitude that counts.

Make it Easier

The activities in this section have been designed to help make out-and-about days easy and fun by focusing on things that are really going to happen.

Where Is Everybody?

These are things that everyone should know to feel comfortable in the world.

While Walking

This is the best time in the world to learn about crossing streets and other rules of the road. It also is a good time to help your child develop a sense of direction. In addition, it can be just plain fun.

While Riding

Teach your child to be a helpful back-seat driver as you go from one place to another. Also, there are more "Sign Games" to play than you will ever have time for.

Personal Data

Materials

- "Personal Data Sheet" (See next page.)
- Pen or pencil

Activity

It is really important for your five-year-old to know her own name, address, telephone number, age, and birth date. If your child should become lost, this is essential information for her to have. It is also just nice to know. We are all more at home in the world if we know who we are and where we belong.

Name

Help your child write her name on the data sheet. Talk about it and repeat it on a daily basis until you are sure this information has been internalized. Have your child practice writing it, with help at first and then independently.

Address

Show your child the number on your house or apartment. Walk out together to see the street sign on the corner. Introduce the concepts of city and state. Show her where these places are on a map. Help write the information on the data sheet. She should practice this as she practiced her name.

Telephone Number

Have your child write her telephone number on the data sheet and practice dialing it on a telephone. (Disconnect the cord on your telephone for this). Whenever you are out and need to call home, let your child place the call. (Teach your child the area code as well.)

Age and Birth Date

Most five-year-olds are well aware of their ages and birthdays. Have your child write this information on the data sheet and add the year.

Personal Data Sheet

NAME

_____

ADDRESS

_____

_____

TELEPHONE NUMBER

_____

AGE AND BIRTH DATE

_____

_____

Personal People

Activity

Materials
- "Personal
  People List"
  (See next
  page.)
- Pen or
  pencil

The "Personal People List" on the next page is for you to fill out and go over with your child. The list is primarily for your child to have. Copies in his room and backpack would be nice. Copies of this list would be handy for his teacher, grandparents, aunts, uncles, and close family friends to have, too.

Go over the list with your child. "This is Mommy's full name, and this is where I am when I go to work. This is my work phone number." Repeat this for each person on the list. Ask your child if there is anyone else who should be on the list.

Perhaps it will be helpful to include other family member names and what they do, including their places of employment and daytime telephone numbers.

Remember to update the list (and all the copies) when the information changes.

Personal People List

Child's Name _____

Address _____

Telephone _____

Mother's Name _____

Place of Business _____

Work Telephone _____

Father's Name _____

Place of Business _____

Work Telephone _____

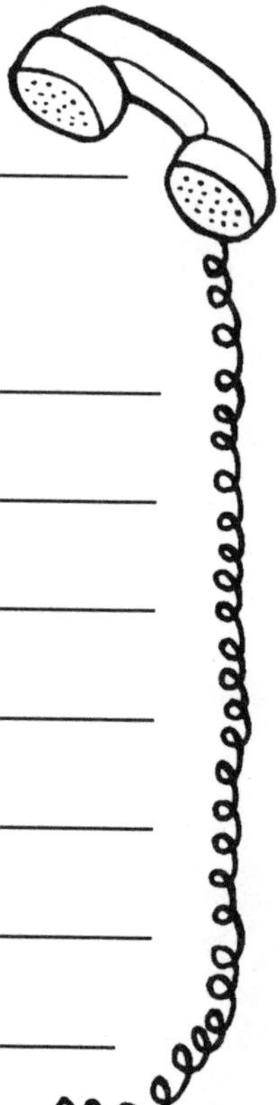

Other Names and Telephone Numbers

_____

_____

_____

_____

_____

_____

Rules of the Road

Activity

Materials

• An area with streets, sidewalks, stop signs, and traffic lights

If possible, start this activity in an area without heavy traffic. If that is not possible, model the activity many times before letting your child take charge.

Take your child on a walk. When you get to an intersection, stop and call his attention to the crosswalk painted on the street. Talk about the word "pedestrian." Discuss the following ideas.

Is there a stop sign? What does it mean? Are there four of them or only two? What does that mean? Is there a stop light? What do the colors mean? If there are special lights for pedestrians, talk about the different symbols on them. What does the hand mean? What does the walking person mean? Is there a button to push?

Most importantly, ask your child, "What should you do before you cross the street?" Teach him the following three rules:

1. STOP: Even if the light is green, you should stop because not all drivers follow the rules. Better safe than sorry!

2. LOOK: You should always look both ways to see what is coming.

3. LISTEN: Even if you can't see anything, you may hear something coming. You also need to listen for sirens because emergency vehicles can go right through red lights if they are on their way to a fire or accident or rushing to get someone to a hospital.

When you feel your child is ready, ask him to be the leader and take you across the street. When you get to an intersection, have your child hold your hand, follow all the rules, and tell you when it is safe to cross.

Finding Places

Activity

Materials

- Short trips with familiar destinations
- Map
- Paper
- Pencils

The ability to visualize where you are in relation to where you are going is a handy skill to have. Some people do this verbally: "Go straight two blocks, turn left and go three blocks. Make a right at the corner by the library." Other people simply have to see it, and so they draw a map, usually with street names written in.

Start this activity by drawing a simple map of your neighborhood. If you live in an area with straight streets that cross at right angles, drawing a map is simple to do. If you live in an area with curvy streets and cul-de-sacs, try to get an already drawn map of the area.

Sometimes, neighborhood schools send home maps like this for the children who are planning to walk to school. Sometimes local realtors have them, too. Or, you might check with your city hall.

Help your child to locate your home on the map and draw an "X" on it. Go outside and hold the map in such a way that you are looking at the street in front of your home and right and left match the way the street runs. Decide on a nearby destination (a friend's house, a neighborhood store, etc.) and, using the street names, mark it on the map. Next, decide on your route, mark it with arrows or a colored marker, and then try it.

Celebrate! Then try it again for as many destinations as you wish. This experience will build your child's ability to follow directions, recognize signs, distinguish right from left, and use a simple map.

Look Up, Look Down

Activity

Half the fun of walking is having time to look around. Where you look determines what you see as much as where you are. Have fun with your five-year-old by seeing things through her eyes.

Make some copies of the "Up and Down Record" on the next page. Take one with you every time you and your five-year-old go walking. As you walk along, say "Look up. Tell me what you see." Write it down for your child. Continue to walk and say, "Look down. Tell me what you see." Write it down.

After a number of walks, read over your five-year-old's "Up and Down Record" with her and talk about the walks you have taken. Put your collected records in a binder and keep adding to it. You will have a journal of the walks you have taken together for a keepsake.

Materials

- Short walking trips in different areas
- "Up and Down Record" (See next page.)
- Pencils

Look Up, Look Down *(cont.)*

UP AND DOWN RECORD

WHERE WE WALKED	WHAT I SAW UP	WHAT I SAW DOWN

Back-Seat Driver

Activity

Materials
• Car trips

Many parents spend a lot of time chauffeuring their children—to and from school, day care, lessons, sports practices, play dates, parties, etc. Stress on the road can lead to accidents, so enlist your five-year-old's help in observing the rules of the road and avoiding the erratic driving behavior of other drivers.

Ask your five-year-old to tell you about traffic signals.

"The light turned yellow. Slow down."

"You've got the green arrow. You can go."

"The light is red up ahead."

Ask your five-year-old to observe boulevard stops.

"This is a four-way stop."

"This is a two-way stop. Watch for traffic."

Ask your five-year-old to warn you about hazards.

"Some kids are playing ball up ahead."

"That woman is jaywalking."

"A man is working in that tree near the street."

Ask your five-year-old to notice other drivers.

"That car is pulling out of the driveway."

"He wants to change lanes. His blinker is on."

Tell your five-year-old not to "help" other people drive. This little secret is just between the two of you!

Sign Games

Activities

Games involving the signs you see along the road are easy to invent on the spur of the moment. You and your five-year-old probably already have favorites of your own. Nevertheless, here are a few suggestions, some of which may be new to you.

Alphabet Game

Find each letter of the alphabet, in order, identifying the place where it was seen. Ideas include road signs, license plates, or billboard advertisements. You can take turns finding alphabet letters or see who can complete his or her own alphabet first. This can be played backwards too, starting with "Z," or with numbers.

Name Game

Spot the letters in order as they appear in your name. Play with your child's name, your name, or a favorite friend or animal's name.

Word Game

Choose a word your five-year-old can spell and find its letters in the order they appear in the word.

Sign Bingo

Prepare cards ahead of time with columns of letters in random order. If you are driving, have your child keep both cards and make an "X" through the letters seen. Win with letters in a horizontal, vertical, or diagonal row, or play "blackout," where the whole card has to be covered.

Singing Games

Activities

Materials

• Any trip in the car

Impromptu songs and singing games, shared while locked in the privacy of your own mobile space, require less preparation and afford more pleasure than do many expensive, planned-ahead-for activities. You're not a singer? You've never been able to carry a tune? You can't remember all of the words? No problem. You will never have a less critical or more appreciative audience than your own five-year-old.

The Alphabet Song

We all know the alphabet song, but try these variations:

The Alternate Alphabet Song

You sing the first letter, your child sings the second, and so on to the end—with many stops for giggles and re-starts along the way. When you finally get it right all the way through, take time to cheer and clap.

The Backwards Alphabet Song

Same tune, same "words," only backwards. (This is harder for adults than it is for kids.) When you finally get to the end, think of an alternative ending that rhymes. Instead of singing, "Now I've sung my ABC's. Next time won't you sing with me?" try "Now "I've sung my CBA's, _____."

Singing Games *(cont.)*

Sally, the Camel

Sally, the Camel is an early childhood version of that old road trip favorite, "99 Bottles of Beer on the Wall" in which you count backwards, only in this song you count backwards from five.

Sally, the camel, had five humps.
Sally, had five humps.
Sally, the camel, had five humps.
So ride, Sally, ride.
Boom, boom, boom, boom!

Repeat the same verse, using four, three, two, and one. Then sing the last verse:

Sally, the camel, had no humps.
Sally, had no humps.
Sally, the camel, had no humps.
'Cause Sally was a horse.
Of course.

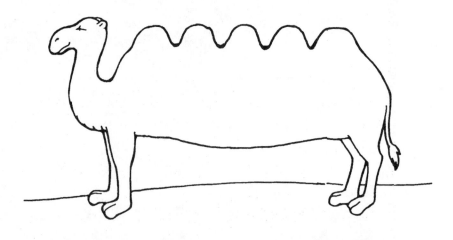

Using a Pay Phone

Activities

Materials
- Pay phone
- Quarter

The ability to use a pay phone is a good skill for a child to have. The experience will take some advance planning on your part, however. Most important is to have someone stationed at home to accept the call. Then you will have to decide on the method you want to use.

Conventional Calls

Have your child always carry a quarter. You can tape one inside each of his pairs of shoes. Your five-year-old can then simply dial the number with a coin deposit.

It is also valuable to teach your child how to dial "0" for operator and say "I want to make a collect call," and then give the number orally, together with his first name. (Most pay phones let you access the operator without first depositing a coin.)

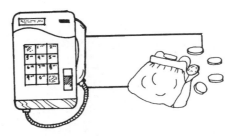

Keeping Up with Technology

If you have a beeper, make sure your child knows that number, as well as the technique for calling a beeper number and leaving the number he is calling from.

If your telephone company has special rules for calling collect, make yourself aware of them so you can explain them to your child.

Teach your child how to use your cellular phone if you use one. In an emergency situation, this skill could be a lifesaver!

Sharing the Cookies

Materials

- Friends
- Cookies
- "Cookie Sheet" (See next page.)
- Paper
- Pen or pencil
- Pennies or buttons

Activity

While out-and-about after school, especially at lessons and practices, there is often a reason to take cookies for a celebration of one kind or another. Maybe someone is having a birthday, or the group had a successful game or performance. If it is your turn to take cookies, let your five-year-old have the fun of figuring out how many you need to take and passing them out when you get there.

Determine the number of people who will be eating cookies. Your child can count the people the week preceding her turn. (You may want to make a telephone call to confirm this number. Don't forget the teacher or coach and yourself.) Have your child write this number on the "Cookie Sheet" on the next page.

Ask your child how many cookies each person should have. How many cookies are usually served? Should you serve the same number or more or less? Have your child write this number on the "Cookie Sheet."

Play the "Cookie Matching Game." Write each person's name on a small piece of paper and lay these out on the table. Use pennies or buttons or any other small item to represent the cookies. Let your five-year-old give each person the number of "cookies" you have decided to serve. Then have your child count the total number of cookies and write the figure on the Cookie Sheet.

Should you have some extra cookies for unexpected people or in case some of the cookies break? Consult your cookie expert, decide on a number, and have it written on the Cookie Sheet. Add that number of cookies to the counting pile and let your five-year-old count again. Show her how to make piles of ten cookies to make the counting easier. Write down the final number.

Sharing the Cookies *(cont.)*

COOKIE SHEET

NUMBER OF PEOPLE _____

COOKIES EACH _____

EXTRA COOKIES _____

TOTAL COOKIES _____

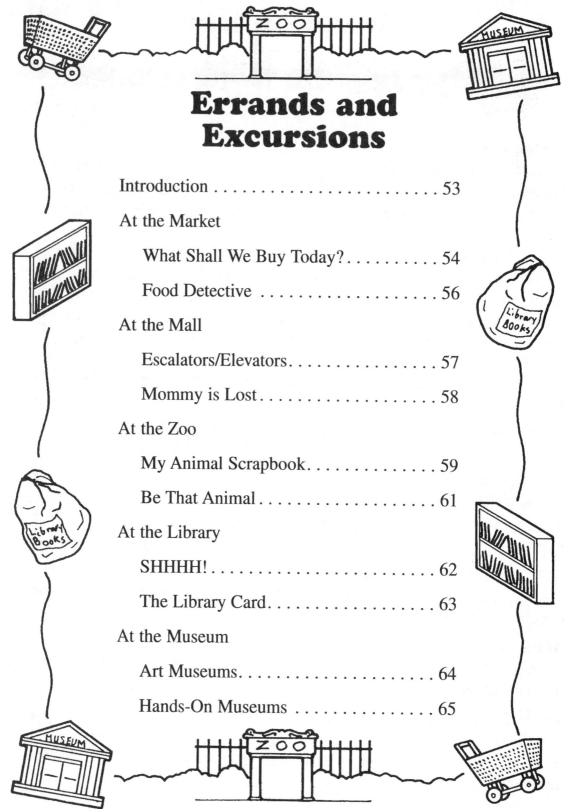

Errands and Excursions

Introduction

Taking Part

While the previous section, "Out-and-About Days," focused primarily on the process of getting places, you do often want to get off the bus or out of the car and go into a place of business. Keeping a five-year-old busy and happy in a store brings a whole new set of challenges. It can even be difficult to keep your visit to a zoo, library, or museum on a positive note. However, it is much easier in the long run to involve your child in what is really going on than to deal with misbehavior arising from boredom.

Parents can easily take some tips from teachers to handle these situations. Teachers often take classes of 30 or more children out in public! They manage these occasions by talking ahead of time about what the children will be seeing and how they will be expected to act. Then they develop some take-along materials that will keep each child focused on and involved in the actual experience. These techniques work just as well for one adult and one child as they do for one adult who is managing a large group.

Make it Easier

The activities in this section have been designed to help make errands and excursions easy and fun by focusing on things that are really going to happen.

At the Market and At the Mall

These are simple activities that help you get ready and make things easier once you get there.

At the Zoo

This is the easiest of all excursions because it is outdoors. Loud voices are not a problem!

At the Library and At the Museum

It is very hard for a five-year-old to talk in a quiet voice and walk along sedately. These activities contain the tips to make it easier and more enjoyable for both of you.

What Shall We Buy Today?

Materials

- "My Grocery List" (See next page.)
- Pencils

Activity

Before you go to the market to buy groceries, sit down with your five-year-old and make your grocery lists. Decide which purchases and how many he can choose. Cereal? Fruit? Lunch items? Help your child write these words and the numbers of items on "My Grocery List" on the next page. If you do this first, the discussion of standards and rules will seem more relevant, and if you decide on the number of items, you won't need to discuss it in the store. ("One box of cereal" is a better list item than just "cereal.")

Agree on some standards for your five-year-old's behavior. No running, yelling, or rudeness come to mind immediately, but you will get farther if you phrase these requirements positively: Quiet walking and talking, and polite behavior and conversation are required. Decide on some shopping rules—whatever you can live with. Will you make your choices first—with your child's help and conversation, of course—and then let your child make his choices if the level of behavior has been up to the standards you set? Or, will you make some choices and then allow your child to make one and so on?

Set off to the market on a positive note. Say something like "It certainly makes shopping easier to have a good helper like you!" and "My, you are sure grown-up!"

What Shall We Buy Today? *(cont.)*

MY GROCERY LIST

1. _____

2. _____

3. _____

4. _____

5. _____

6. _____

7. _____

8. _____

Food Detective

Materials

- Small pad of paper
- Pen or pencil

Activity

Is your five-year-old a "food-fussy?" Does she exist on a diet of hot dogs, bologna sandwiches, peanut butter, and an occasional banana or apple? Maybe you can challenge your child to at least think about trying something new!

Supply your shopping companion with a small pad of paper (a thick one that doesn't bend when it is written on will be best) and a pen or pencil.

Ask your child to find five foods that she has never tried and write their names on the pad of paper. If you are in the produce department, point out how the names of the fruits and vegetables are displayed above or below the bins that hold them. A picture of the food might help, too. Ask your child to draw one next to the name.

Don't look at the list until you get home. You don't want your child to think you are going to actually try any of these new foods.

Look over the list together. Talk about the foods. Look them up in an encyclopedia. Does your child know that people who eat broccoli are actually eating flowers? Or that peanuts grow underground? Or that pineapple comes from Hawaii?

If your child shows any interest in trying a new food, agree (reluctantly) to think about buying it next time. Good luck!

Escalators/Elevators

Activities

Materials

• Mall with escalators and elevators

Escalators and elevators are a routine part of life to most adults, but they are still a source of delight to children who seem to think of them as rides in an amusement park. You can use this fact of life to teach a few safety lessons and give your child an experience in self-reliance and independence.

Try these activities the next time you go to the mall:

1. Find the elevator and let your child push the button. When you get in, let him select the floor and push that button, too. Ride all the way up and all the way down at least once. Show your child how to hold the door open so it won't shut on anyone. If your mall has a glass elevator, be sure to try it, too.

2. Go up and down as many escalators as you have time for or can stand. Insist that your five-year-old hold the handrail as he steps on and off, and stands still, holding on during the ride.

3. While at the mall, try to spot a place where there are up and down escalators side by side. Help your child develop skill and confidence in riding ascending and descending escalators by showing him when and how to step on and off safely.

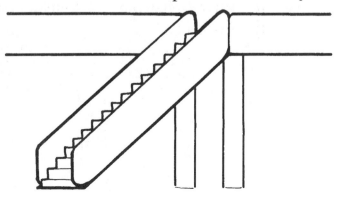

Mommy is Lost

Activity

Materials

• Mall with security guards and/or an information desk

Most children never get lost. However, once in awhile a little one gets confused in a mall, loses sight of her adult, and needs to find some help.

Find the information desk in your local mall and ask the person who works there what their procedure is for helping lost children. Explain these procedures to your child and show her how to find the desk by looking for a familiar landmark. ("See. There's the toy store where we bought your doll.")

Next, locate a security guard. Introduce yourself and your child and explain that you are making sure your child knows how to find help if she ever needs it. Call attention to the kind of uniform the guard is wearing so your child will be able to identify the right person to ask for help.

Tell your child how to attract the attention of the adult at the desk or begin a conversation with the security guard. (Children's comments like these will almost always attract help. "Excuse me. Could you help me, please?")

You can also designate a special place where you can always go to meet one another in case you get separated. ("You can always wait for me on the bench by the fountain.") This is best, though, when you stick to one store or area of the mall. Looking for a special area in a large mall can be overwhelming for a lost or confused child.

Since some children find all this information upsetting, talk a lot about holding hands and always staying together.

My Animal Scrapbook

Activity

Handle your next trip to the zoo like a school field trip. Brief your child ahead of time and supply materials that will keep a five-year-old focused on the experience.

Before going to the zoo, get some books on zoos and zoo animals and read together about what you might see. Talk about where the animals live in the wild, which ones are endangered, and anything else about the animals that your five-year-old finds interesting.

Encourage your child to talk about some of the animals as you walk through the zoo.

Stop in the gift shop on the way out and buy postcard pictures of the animals your child particularly enjoyed seeing.

When you get home, mount a postcard in the space at the top of the "My Animal Scrapbook" form. On the lines below the picture, have your child dictate to you what he recalls about the animal in the photo. Three-hole punch the completed forms and insert them in a binder. Mount the postcards on plain pieces of paper and insert them in the binder, too, where they will best illustrate the notes your child made.

Add the new scrapbook to your child's library and read it over occasionally, reviewing what you learned about the animals and discussing how much fun you had at the zoo.

Materials

- Several copies of the "My Animal Scrapbook" form (See next page.)
- Pencils
- Postcards
- Three-ring binder

My Animal Scrapbook *(cont.)*

Animal _____

_____

_____

_____

_____

Be That Animal

Materials

- Zoo Book from pages 59–60

Activity

This is a follow-up activity to your zoo excursion and will provide an enjoyable activity for some empty time. Use it when you get ready too early and have to wait, or during any other time that needs to be filled with something entertaining. (Teachers call these "sponge" activities.)

Get out the Zoo Book with your child's zoo notes in it. Hide your eyes while your child flips through the book to find an animal to imitate. Have your five-year-old pretend to be the animal. Guess which animal is being portrayed. If you are right, your child gets to be another animal. If you are wrong, it is your turn. (Or, it can continue to be your child's turn. You don't have to play. You can continue to be the audience. Just be sure to clap a lot!) Invite other members of the family to participate, too. Many hidden talents may be discovered, and everyone is sure to have fun.

SHHHH!

Materials

• Library

Activities

Some five-year-olds really do not know how to whisper. Some can whisper and, indeed, start out whispering, but their excitement runs away with them. Being excited about books in a library is just what we all want for our children, so we need to give them some whispering practice.

Libraries are not the totally silent places they used to be. Some libraries encourage children to talk quietly. Nevertheless, it is still good to at least know how to whisper, just in case.

Demonstrate whispering for your child. Have her imitate you. This can be a pretty silly game, so take time out to giggle and then practice some more.

Have a family whisper day. Ask everyone to whisper all day.

Show your child how to get your attention without raising her voice. Agree on a signal you can use in public, maybe a tug on your sleeve.

Review and practice whispering in the car or bus on the way to the library.

Don't stay too long! Find the books you want and leave before the whispering becomes a strain.

After a successful library visit, go somewhere your child can yell!

The Library Card

Activity

Materials
• Library

The day a child gets his very own library card is an exciting one. Checking out books is fun! Reading the books or hearing them read is wonderful! The hard part is taking the books back. You can help the whole library experience to remain exciting by helping your child set up a system for getting the books back on time.

Take your five-year-old to get a library card. In most libraries, the child is asked to write his own name to get the card. Practice before you go. Treat this privilege with the respect it deserves. Maybe a gift of a wallet to hold the library card would be appropriate.

Give your child a wall calendar to hang in his room. Have him mark the day the books are due to be returned. A capital "L" for library works, or the word "Books." Help your five-year-old clear a shelf in his room to hold just library books. Check to see that they are always returned to that spot. Make yourself available to go to the library before the books become overdue. Ask your child to remind you by looking at his calendar.

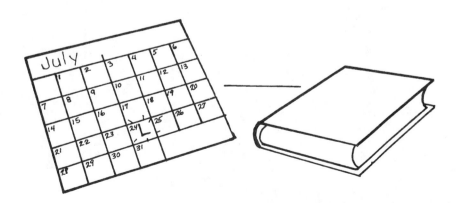

Art Museums

Activity

Nothing increases a child's vocabulary like a new experience. If your five-year-old has never been to an art museum, you may wish to try it. Talk about it ahead of time. Tell your child that there will be large empty rooms with paintings on the walls, as well as rooms full of statues. (Describe the statues vividly because some children find them scary.)

Find one picture or statue that is your child's favorite. Talk about why she likes it best. Write down its name, as well as the name of the artist. Go to the museum gift shop and see if you can get a postcard or other small reproduction of it. Be sure to display your child's momento of her favorite piece of art for the rest of the family and let her talk about your excursion.

Make your first visit short. See just a few things and talk about them. Leave before anyone (you or your five-year-old) gets tired and cross.

Materials
• Museum

Hands-On Museums

Materials

• Hands-on museum

Activity

Hands-on museums were once devoted mostly to science exhibits, or else they were child-centered experiences with arts and crafts and opportunities for dress-up play. Now many natural history museums have added hands-on exhibits that appeal to everyone.

Find out what is at the museum before you venture out. A telephone call can get you a lot of information. They may even send you some brochures about their current exhibits. Take the time to learn something about what you will see before you go. Go over any materials with your child or get some books from the library. Dinosaur exhibits are particularly fascinating, and your child will be even more interested if he already has some information. Don't try to see everything in one visit. See just enough so your child will be eager to go back. Take home all the free materials you can get so you can remember what you saw and plan your next trip. If you go to the gift shop, a dinosaur coloring book is an excellent thing to buy. It won't be long before your child knows all of the dinosaurs and their names and you know more about dinosaurs than you ever wanted to know!

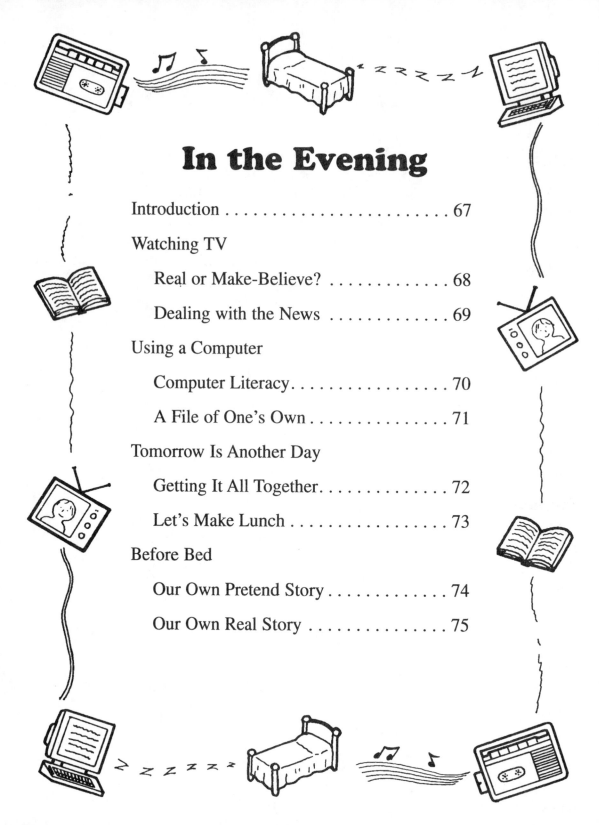

In the Evening

Introduction

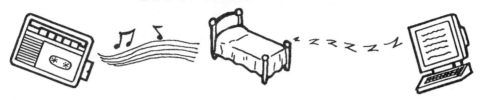

Home at Last

Evenings, like mornings, can be awful or wonderful, the best or the worst part of the day. After an at-home day or an out-and-about day full of errands and excursions, what is nicer than snuggling up on the sofa and looking at a little TV? "Oh, no," you say, "not TV!" But TV is, after all, a fact of modern life. And you can make it a plus rather than a minus in the life of your five-year-old simply by sharing it. Or, maybe you would rather spend some time with a computer, another facet of modern life. Share that with your five-year-old, too.

And, after all of the technology is taken care of, try some old-fashioned bedtime stories, both real and make-believe. The stress will simply melt away—guaranteed!

Make It Easier

The activities in this section have been designed to help make your evenings easy and fun by focusing on things that are really going to happen.

Watching TV

Say the right thing at the right time, and your child will absorb your values rather than those of some media personality. Say the right thing at the right time, and your child will learn to distinguish between real and make-believe, good and bad.

Using a Computer

Send your child off to school with the vocabulary and skills needed to be computer competent, as well as computer literate.

Getting It All Together

Help your child build responsibility skills as you spend time together getting ready for the upcoming day.

Before Bed

Make your own magic with some unique bedtime stories that will end the day on a happy note for both you and your child.

Real or Make-Believe?

Activities

Materials
- TV programs

Snuggling up on the sofa to watch TV with a trusted adult is a very different experience from watching by yourself, especially when you are five years old. Try conversation starters like these:

- Cartoons are make-believe. That's what makes them funny. Nothing bad can really happen in a cartoon because the characters are just drawings.

- The reason that people think it's funny when kids do naughty things on TV programs is because those things are not funny in real life, and people don't really do them. A food fight that looks funny on TV would be disgusting in real life. Everybody would have to clean up all the mess, and no one would laugh. On TV, actors get paid to do those things, and other people clean up the mess.

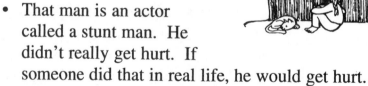

- That man is an actor called a stunt man. He didn't really get hurt. If someone did that in real life, he would get hurt.

- Play "Real or Make-Believe." Watch a program together. Take turns asking "Real or make-believe?" Talk about how you can tell.

- If something looks real, decide if it is being done by an actor or a real person. Talk about how you can tell.

These experiences will help your child develop the ability to distinguish between what is real and what is make-believe.

Dealing with the News

Activity

People worry a great deal about violence on TV, but sometimes they tend to forget that children see more violence on the news than they see on programs designed to entertain. Pictures of war, especially, are very upsetting to small children, as are pictures of disasters, both natural and man-made.

How can parents explain what children see, especially in the context of teaching what is real and what is make-believe? If something is real, one must deal with the idea of good and bad. Try some of these ideas with your five-year-old:

- If something is on the news, it is unusual. Something that is unusual does not happen very often. Bad things and bad people are unusual. That is why they are on the news.
- Good things happen all the time. Most people are very good. Good things and good people are not news because there are so many of them. They aren't considered "news."
- Those pictures that you just saw were of something that is happening far away. It is not happening here. Maybe we can do something to help those people. Let's find out what we can do.
- If something bad were to happen here, I would take care of you. You are very important to me. I will protect you.

Computer Literacy

Materials

• Computer keyboard or facsimile

Activities

In many schools, even the kindergartners are expected to be working on computers. A little familiarity with the computer as a tool will make life easier for your five-year-old.

If you have a computer at home, your child can experiment with the real thing. If you don't have a computer, you can find a facsimile computer keyboard at a teacher supply store. It isn't quite as much fun, but it will serve the purpose and give your five-year-old a good head start in school.

Play "Find the Space bar." (The space bar is an important key to know if you are using children's software.)

Play "Find the Enter (or Return) Key." (Explain to your child that the computer doesn't know what you want to do in many cases until you press this key.)

Play "Write Your Name." (Press each letter of your name in order and then press "Return." You can also play "Write the ABC's.")

Play "Move with the Arrows." (Move up and down, and left and right with the arrows—another basic move in using children's software. Explain to your child that the arrows may be in different places on different keyboards.)

Play "Find the Shift Key." (Explain about the upper and lowercase letters.)

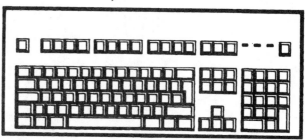

A File of One's Own

Activities

Materials
- Computer
- Word processing program
- Printer

Give your five-year-old real ownership of important computer skills by making her own file. Demonstrate how to save the file and how to get back into it.

Begin by opening a file for your child. Give it her name for easy identification on the menu. Let your child write whatever she wants to—strings of letters and/or numbers, her name, or familiar words such as "zoo," "stop," and "no." (Using a large font will make the letters easier for her to see.) You can also dictate some words. Be ready to supply letters as needed.

Have your five-year-old tell you a story as you enter the words. Read it together a few times. Be sure to save the file. Next time the file is opened, see if she remembers the story and read it again. It will help to point to each word as it is read.

When your child writes words, sentences, or a story of her own, print it. Start a folder or binder of these stories. Date them and keep them in order so your child can look at the progress that is being made over a period of time. In school, this is called a "portfolio."

When your five-year-old needs to write a thank-you note, make the computer and printer available for the project. You will have a polite child who is having fun at the same time. Demonstrate the use of the "spell check," too, and you will soon have a speller, as well as a writer!

Getting It All Together

Materials

- Clothes
- Calendar
- Chair
- Large doll or teddy bear

Activities

Help your child become more responsible by preparing for each day the night before.

What's Happening Tomorrow?

Hang up a calendar at eye-level in your child's room. Mark the days for school and other events such as dance class, T-ball practice, and church. Each night, before bed, help your child find the date on the calendar and look at what is happening the next day. If there are two events— school and dance class, for example, get ready for both things the night before.

Make a Kid Chair

Place a chair where your child can reach it. Help her hang a shirt or dress (on its hanger to prevent wrinkles) on the back of the chair. Place pants on the seat of the chair with the legs hanging down. Shoes go right below the pants' legs with socks stuffed in them. Underwear can go on top of the pants. Outerwear can be draped over the back of the chair.

For more fun, draw a picture of a cute face and mount it on cardboard, or mount an enlarged picture of your child's face and attach it to the back of the chair.

Dress a Doll or Bear-Wear

Sit an over-sized doll or teddy bear on a chair and help your child drape the clothes in the appropriate places. This is a good place for dance clothes or a baseball uniform. Be sure to find and include the appropriate shoes (tap shoes, ballet slippers, cleats, etc.), socks, and accessories. This pre-planning is bound to make getting ready to leave a more pleasant experience for everyone!

Let's Make Lunch

Materials

- Lunch box foods
- Zipper lock bags
- Lunch box or paper bag

Activities

Make stressful evenings more enjoyable by preparing the next day's lunches together.

The Lunch Box

A lunch box is a major purchase for a five-year-old, if lunch boxes are considered the "in" thing to have at her school. (Sometimes, it is better, socially, to have a paper bag. Using paper bags for lunch also avoids the trauma of the lost lunch box.) If you decide to go with a lunch box, let your child pick it out. If you pick it out, it is almost a certainty that you will get the wrong one and destroy your child's image!

The Food

If you don't mind spending a little extra money for the sake of convenience, individually boxed and packaged foods make lunches easy for a five-year-old to put together. If you want, you can make sandwiches ahead of time, put them in zipper lock bags, and freeze them. Add the frozen sandwich to the lunch in the morning. It will keep the rest of the lunch cool and be thawed by lunch time.

The Process

You can set up some simple guidelines for your five-year-old and even post a chart in the kitchen:

- one sandwich
- one drink in a box or thermos of milk
- one bag of chips
- one piece of fruit
- one dessert

(Enclose a note from you occasionally to make lunch time more fun.)

Our Own Pretend Story

Materials

- Warm, cozy bed

Activity

Make bedtime something to look forward to by inventing an original, pretend story with your five-year-old.

Tell your child that the two of you are going to make up your very own pretend story and that it will go on and on, night after night. Decide on your main character or characters and give them names. Discuss and agree on the names of new characters as they enter the story. Decide where your characters will live and what the place will look like. Decide what the first adventure will be and begin to tell the story. Let your child share in the creative process by interjecting ideas as you go along. Stop for the night at some exciting place, or, if that seems overly stimulating for your child, bring the story to a safe conclusion before stopping.

Begin each night's installment of the story with a recap of what has already happened. It will also help to write down the names of the characters and the outline of their adventures and refer to it now and then. Read it over if there is a gap in your storytelling.

Our Own Real Story

Materials

- Warm, cozy bed
- Tape recorder (Optional)

Activity

Your child will love hearing the real story of his life. You can start with his birth or go back and paint a background story of parents and grandparents. Or, you can start with "today" and make your story a kind of oral journal. You can bring in the past, if you want to, by saying something like, "Today reminded me of the time when . . ." If you spent the day in different places doing different things, take turns with the story. If you take the first turn, you will find that your child will model his storytelling style after yours, so think ahead of time about how you want to start. If you want to, you can record your story each night and create an oral history that will be a treasure in years to come. If you decide to record, be sure to label and date the tapes, or they will be useless to you if you want to find a particular episode. Also, play back a little each night before going on. This will remind both of you to tell about how something that happened the previous day turned out.

Ask another family member to tell the story some nights. Your child will have a chance to see life from more than one point of view and will learn something about the guest storyteller.

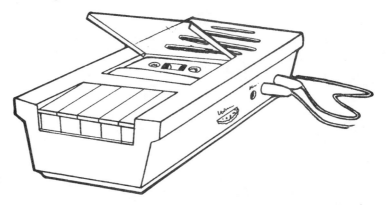

Bibliography of Resources

Brazelton, M.D., & T. Berry. *To Listen to a Child.* Addison Wesley, 1984.

Brazelton, M.D., & T. Berry. *Touchpoints.* Addison Wesley, 1992.

Chapman, W.D., & M. Weston. *Playing Parenting: Turning the Dilemma of Discipline into Fun and Games.* Tarcher/Perigee, 1993.

Chernofsky, B. & D. Gage. *Changing Your Child's Behavior by Changing Yours: 13 New Tricks to Get Kids to Cooperate.* Crown Trade Paperbacks, 1996.

Ellison, S. & J. Gray. *365 Days of Creative Play.* Sourcebooks, Inc., 1995.

Faber, A. & E. Mazlish. *How To Talk So Kids Can Learn.* Rawson Associates, 1995.

Leach, P. *Children First.* Random House, 1994.

MacGregor, C. *Raising a Creative Child.* Carol Publishing Group, 1996.

Rich, D. *MegaSkills.* Houghton Mifflin Company, 1992.

Ziglar, Z. *Raising Positive Kids in a Negative World.* Oliver-Nelson Books, 1985.

Bibliography of Children's Books

Aliki. *Digging Up Dinosaurs.* HarperCollins Publishers, 1988.

Allen, C. *Happy and Sad, Grouchy and Glad.* A Sesame Street/Golden Press Book, 1992.

Asch, F. *Happy Birthday, Moon.* Simon & Schuster, 1988.

Base, G. *Animalia.* Harry N. Abrams, Inc., 1986.

Brown, M.W. *The Color Kittens.* A Golden Book, 1994.

Carle, E. *The Very Busy Spider.* Putman, 1984.

Carle, E. *The Very Hungry Caterpillar.* Putman, 1987.

Carle, E. *The Very Quiet Cricket.* Putman, 1985.

Cherry, L. *The Great Kapok Tree.* Harcourt Brace & Company, 1990.

Dedieu, T. *Baby Clown.* Hyperion Books for Children, 1995.

Dowdy, L.C. *Barney Goes to the Zoo.* The Lyons Group, 1993.

Dowdy, L.C. *Happy Birthday Baby Bop!* The Lyons Group, 1993.

Dudko, M.A., & M. Larsen. *Barney's Color Surprise.* The Lyons Group, 1993.

Dudko, M.A., & M. Larsen. *Where Are My Shoes?* The Lyons Group, 1993.

Eastman, P.D. *Are You My Mother?* Random House, 1960.

Freeman, D. *Corduroy.* Puffin, 1976.

Hill, E. *Spot's Big Book of Words.* Putman, 1968.

Lester, H. *A Porcupine Named Fluffy.* Houghton Mifflin Company, 1986.

Monsell, M.E. *Underwear!* Albert Whitman & Company, 1988.

Munsch, R. *Thomas' Snowsuit.* Annick Press Ltd., 1985.

Numeroff, L.J. *If You Give a Moose a Muffin.* HarperCollins Publishers, 1991.

Scarry, R. (Every title by Richard Scarry is worth reading!)

Seuss, Dr. (Every title by Dr. Seuss is a must!)

Wormser, D. *Hippity Hop, It's Baby Bop!* The Lyons Groups, 1995.

Zion, G. *Harry the Dirty Dog.* HarperCollins Publishers, 1956.

Bibliography of Music Videos

Alvin and the Chipmunks. *Working on the Railroad.* Buena Vista Home
Video.

Barney, The Lyons Group. All of the Barney videos are excellent. A few
examples follow:
Barney's Alphabet Soup
Barney's Alphabet Zoo
Barney's Birthday
Barney's Imagination Island
Barney in Concert
Barney Live in New York City
Barney's Magical Musical Adventure
Barney's Mother Goose
Barney's Waiting for Santa

Carle, E. *The Very Hungry Caterpillar and Other Stories.* Disney Home
Video, 1995.

Scarry, R. *Richard Scarry's Best Learning Songs Video Ever.* Random
House, 1993.

Scarry, R. *Richard Scarry's Best Sing-Along Mother Goose.* Random
House, 1994.

Scarry, R. *Richard Scarry's Best Silly Songs Video Ever.* Random House,
1995.

Sesame Street, Jim Henson Productions, Inc. All of the Sesame Street
videos are excellent. Examples include the following:
Bedtime Stories
Dance Along!
It's Not Easy Being Green
A Musical Celebration
Sing, Hoot & Howl

Sing Along Songs, Disney. This series is excellent, too! Try these:
Colors of the Wind
Heigh-Ho
Laughing Place
Supercalifragilisticexpialidocious
The Twelve Days of Christmas